Introducti◌

The first Local Walks Guide to Mac... 1995, and has proved popular with ... alike. The town's magnificent sitt... between the Plynlimons and Snowdonia, a ... coast, makes it an excellent centre for walkers, who can enjoy some of Wales' finest countryside. It is with this firmly in mind that we have produced this *second* book of local walks, encompassing both the north and south sides of the lower Dyfi Valley, as far as the popular seaside resorts of Aberdyfi and Borth.

All of the walks can be undertaken by a reasonably fit person, with **Walk 15** being the most demanding. Walking boots or stout shoes are recommended for all the walks, and an anorak is a sensible idea if the weather is changeable. A weather forecast can be obtained by calling 0891 505315 (charge). *And remember always* that this is sheep farming country − if you wish to be accompanied by your dog, *you must keep it on a lead at all times.*

The location of each walk is shown on the back cover, and a summary of the key characteristics of each is given opposite. All of the routes follow public rights of way, permissive paths or Forestry Commission tracks, and have been recently checked. Things do change rapidly however, so don't always assume you have lost your way if what you find differs from the information in this book. Instructions to reach the start of each walk are given from the Clock Tower in Machynlleth. A short way along Maengwyn Street is the Tourist Information Centre (01654 702401), an excellent source of local visitor information, with details of accommodation in the area. There are other equally useful Tourist Information Centres in Aberdyfi and Borth, which are open in season.

Please always respect local traditions, and care for the environment, so that all those who wish to share the great charm and beauty of this area may continue to do so.

About the author, David Perrott . . .

Having moved with his wife Morag to Machynlleth from London some twenty years ago, his love of this area remains as strong now as it was then. A member of the local Ramblers' group, he still enjoys walking and cycling around Machynlleth which, lying on the southern border of the Snowdonia National Park, still remains remarkably unspoilt and undiscovered.

WALK 1
ABERDYFI PANORAMA

DESCRIPTION This gentle hilly 3½-mile walk soon gets you up above Aberdyfi, enjoying fine views over the mouth of the Dyfi estuary and south towards Borth and Aberystwyth. The descent is through a very pretty cwm (valley), followed by a path along the dunes. Allow 2 hours.
START The Tourist Information Centre, Aberdyfi. SN 614959.

DIRECTIONS From the Clock Tower in Machynlleth, take the A487 north to cross the Dyfi Bridge and turn left onto the A493. Continue to Aberdyfi, where there is a large car park on the left, just beyond the Tourist Information Centre. Or you can take the excellent train journey from Machynlleth to Aberdyfi. Bus 29 from Machynlleth to Aberdyfi operates Mon-Sat.

Turn sharp RIGHT here and climb steeply up this path. Continue ahead when the path widens and becomes a tarmac road. Continue along the road, passing between houses to join another road.

1 From the Tourist Information Centre walk to the RIGHT, then take the first LEFT into Copperhill Street. Continue up the street, passing under the railway bridge.

2 After the third house beyond the railway bridge, take the path to the LEFT, which climbs uphill, and is joined by a path from the right just after No 2 Bryniau-Isaf.

3 Cross this road, and then cross the ladder stile opposite. Turn LEFT, following the direction indicated by the arrow. *As you climb, superb coastal views open up.* The path follows the edge of the field, climbing gently, then quite steeply, to reach a stile.

4 Cross the stile, and continue with a fence to your left. Cross another stile in the corner of the field, and carry on ahead, following the yellow waymark arrows, to eventually descend to the footpath arrow to the right-hand side of *Trefeddian Farm*. Cross the small stream by the sign and turn LEFT following the direction indicated to walk around the back of the farm buildings. Go through the waymarked gateway, pass through a gateway ahead, then turn RIGHT through the next gate, which is again waymarked. After about 15 yards, look down to your LEFT, to locate a small footbridge over a stream, with a stile just beyond. Descend to the stream and cross them both.

5 From the stile, walk ahead, uphill, for about 10 yards to reach a small brow. Turn LEFT here, following the narrow path. At the handsome, but derelict, stone buildings of *Trefeddian-fach* continue ahead, following the path between low summits. The path now becomes a tarmac lane, which you follow down through Cwm Safn-ast.

6 Pass through a gate, opposite the cemetery, to join the coast road. Cross the road, veering slightly RIGHT, to go down another track to the railway. Pass through the gates and CAREFULLY cross the railway, looking and listening for trains. Continue along the track to a T junction. *You are now on Aberdyfi Golf Course, so watch out for fast moving golf balls.* Turn LEFT at the path junction, following the track until it veers away to the right. At this point continue ahead, keeping parallel with the railway. Eventually you join another track. Follow this, ignoring the first waymark sign to the left, which points across the railway.

7 Just beyond the Trefeddian Hotel, which is over the railway and road to your left, you will see a railway level crossing. Turn left and follow the track to this, and cross it carefully, again looking and listening for trains. Join the main road and turn RIGHT to return to the Tourist Information Centre.

*A*berdyfi *is a pretty resort village in an enviable situation, facing south across the Dyfi estuary and sheltered by steep hills to the north. It is well known for the folk song 'The Bells of Aberdovey', composed around 1785 by Charles Dibdin, and featured in his Drury Lane musical 'Liberty Hall'. The bells now lie under the sea with Cantre'r Gwaelod, the Lowland Hundred, which was at one time a low fertile plain protected by sea walls, supporting several villages and towns. In legend the sea walls were in the care of Prince Seithennin, a warrior of Lord Gwyddno Garanhir, and this was unfortunate, as Seithennin's main preoccupation was with feasting and drinking, rendering him drunk most of the time. Eventually, during the sixth century, the inevitable south-westerly gale coincided with a high tide. Seithennin had let maintenance slip and the walls were breached: the land disappeared beneath the waves, never to be reclaimed. It may well have been that all the activity in the region did take place to the west of Aberdyfi, since in 1569 it was recorded that there were only three dwellings in here, even though herring fleets often sought shelter in the estuary.*

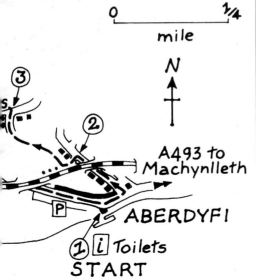

0 — ¼

mile

N

A493 to Machynlleth

ABERDYFI

① ⓘ Toilets
START

WALK 2
ABOVE PICNIC ISLAND

DESCRIPTION The effort involved in the initial climb on this 4-mile walk is repaid many times over by stunning views over the Dyfi estuary and the whole sweep of Cardigan Bay, from Bardsey in the north to Strumble Head, Pembrokeshire, in the south. The last ¼ mile, given suitable tides, includes the Roman Road. Allow 2½ hours. **START** The lay-by at Picnic Island, on the A493 between Machynlleth and Aberdyfi. SN 626963.

DIRECTIONS From the Clock Tower in Machynlleth, take the A487 north to cross the Dyfi Bridge and turn left onto the A493 towards Aberdyfi. After about 9½ miles look out for the clearly signposted 'Outward Bound Wales' on the right. Park in the next lay-by on the left, at the entrance to Picnic Island. Or you can take the train from Machynlleth to Penhelig Station and start the walk from there. Bus 29 from Machynlleth to Aberdyfi operates Mon–Sat.

1 From Picnic Island, walk to the RIGHT along the road for about 100 yards to reach a footpath sign on the north side of the road, just before the entrance to the Outward Bound. Following the direction indicated by the sign, cross the stone wall and walk up the path beside a stream. Cross the footbridge, climb steps, cross the ladder stile and continue. After about 20 yards turn sharp LEFT, following the footpath arrow, and climb steps to arrive at the Outward Bound rope course. Continue uphill and, by a large tractor tyre suspended in a tree, turn right to cross a stile. Now walk half-RIGHT along the rear of the buildings, then head gently uphill, passing an old corrugated iron garage building, to reach a footpath sign.

2 DO NOT follow the direction (left) indicated by the sign, but continue ahead, walking gently uphill along a pleasant grassy track. *Pause at the first summit to look back over the estuary, and enjoy the first of many fine views on this walk.* When the track veers left DO NOT follow it, but continue ahead, starting to descend towards trees. A path appears, and soon you arrive at a well hidden Llwybr Cyhoeddus (footpath) sign. Continue in the direction indicated. Gradually the path descends more steeply (take care!) to a ladder stile in the corner.

3 Cross the stile and turn left to walk along a tarmac lane, crossing a cattle grid and continuing up the lane to *Trefrifawr*. Enter the yard, walk to the right of the house and

follow the direction indicated on the footpath sign, to reach a stile.

4 Cross the stile and continue along the path uphill, with a stream to your right. Eventually you come to a ladder stile. Cross it and follow the track, which veers to the right. Cross a farm track and continue ahead, to reach a tarmac lane.

5 Turn LEFT to walk along the lane. *On a clear day the Lleyn Peninsula can be seen stretching along the horizon to Bardsey Island. Soon the view encompasses the whole of Cardigan Bay, as far south as Strumble Head.* Eventually the lane begins to descend, and another lane joins from the left.

6 Turn left into this lane and walk downhill. Go through a gate and continue for about 20 yards to a waymarked double gate on the right. Go through the gates and walk half-RIGHT down the hill, looking for a waymark post about 100 yards down. Locate the post and walk in the direction indicated, to a gap in a hedge with another waymark post (the waymark is on the other side, but there is a smudge of yellow paint). Go through the gap, turn right and walk to the next post. Cross the stile below it, step over the stream and turn LEFT, walking downhill beside the stream, to another stile.

7 Cross this stile and walk down towards the stream and trees. Follow the path, which climbs gently. When you reach a stile, cross it and continue along the path. When you reach a short wooden post with the remains of a footpath sign on it, the path starts to descend. Follow the path, cross a stile and continue along a path now sheltered by a tangle of blackberry and broom.

8 The path finally descends steps beside houses to join a road. Turn right, then immediately left, to continue the descent. When you reach the road, turn left.

9 Just before the railway crosses over the road, opposite the Penhelig Hotel, turn RIGHT to walk by the river.

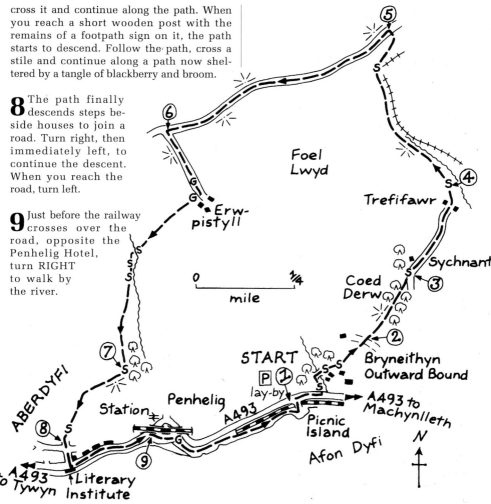

When you rejoin the main road, you have a choice of routes to return to Picnic Island. *If the tides are favourable* – either low or falling – you can turn immediately right to go through a metal gate, and follow the old Roman Road back to Picnic Island. But do take care, as *at certain states of the tide parts of this path can be covered; it can also be slippery when wet; and young children need to be carefully watched if the tide is high.* **If you are at all unsure**, then return to the start of the walk along the road. If you have walked along the Roman Road, climb the steps at Picnic Island, cross the bridge over the railway, and return to your car.

The railway between Dovey Junction and Aberdyfi was constructed in 1867 at great expense, as the residents of Aberdyfi insisted it passed through the village in two tunnels, to remain hidden. The spoil from these tunnels was dumped by the foreshore at Penhelig, and Penhelig Terrace was subsequently built on top. The station here was an afterthought, being built in 1933.

WALK 3
LLYN BARFOG
THE BEARDED
LAKE

DESCRIPTION A short and popular 2½ mile walk from Happy Valley which soon gets you up in the hills enjoying the charms of this lake, with its legendary associations. This is followed by exciting views over the Dyfi estuary on your return. Allow 2 hours.
START From the Snowdonia National Park car park in Happy Valley. SN 641986.
DIRECTIONS From the Clock Tower in Machynlleth, take the A487 north to cross the Dyfi Bridge and turn left onto the A493. When you reach Cwrt, about 5 miles from Machynlleth, fork right onto the road signposted 'Cwm Maethlon – Happy Valley'. After 3½ miles turn left into the car park for the Bearded Lake (look out for the sign, it is easily missed from this direction!).

Cross another gate and ladder-stile and follow the track.

2 When the track bears to the left, follow the direction indicated by the sign along a grassy path. This path soon rejoins the track. Continue ahead to pass through the next gate and ladder-stile *noting the old 'hand-post' sign to Towyn here, and the fine view to the west.* The track climbs uphill to another gate and ladder-stile, which you cross to reach Llyn Barfog, the Bearded Lake. Go through a small gate to gain easy access to the water's edge. *There is a fine view from the cairn on the eastern side. The lake is in a beautifully isolated situation, its surface covered in water-lilies from late June until September. This may have given it its name, although those more romantically inclined would rather it were named in honour of one of King Arthur's knights – in particular 'the bearded one'. Barfog may have even been Arthur's foster father. There is also, not surprisingly, a fairy-tale associated with the lake, concerning a magical cow which came*

1 Leave the car park by the gate in the far right-hand corner, turn LEFT and walk along the track, which curves past farm buildings. When you reach a gate and ladder-stile, cross them and continue ahead.

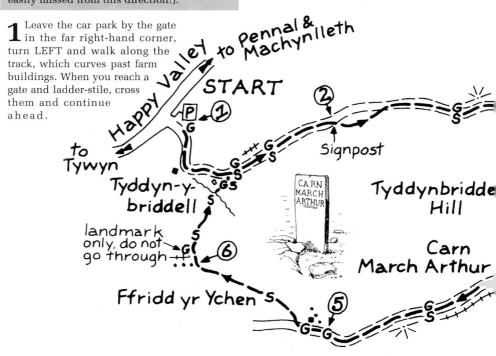

to Pennal & Machynlleth

Happy Valley

START

to Tywyn

Tyddyn-y-briddell

landmark only, do not go through

Ffridd yr Ychen

Signpost

CARN MARCH ARTHUR

Tyddynbridde Hill

Carn March Arthur

into the possession of a farmer of Dysyrnant, half-a-mile to the north. This beast gave birth to many fine calves, and provided many gallons of creamy milk. The farmer, as a consequence, became rich. But eventually the cow grew too old, and the farmer decided to employ a butcher to slaughter her. But as the butcher was about to kill the cow, the knife fell from his hand. A little green fairy woman appeared from by the lake, and called the cow, and her calves, home. The fairy and the cows then disappeared into the lake. From then on the farmer's luck changed for the worse.

3 After enjoying your stay at the lake, retrace your steps through the small gate and, about 100 yards from the edge of the lake, turn LEFT along a green path, indicated by a prominent post on the skyline between two low summits. Continue along the green path, eventually veering RIGHT to join a track, *which is part of the Panorama Walk.*

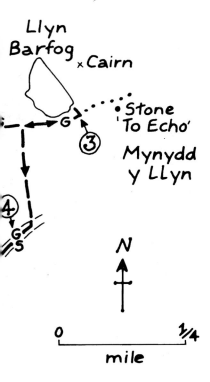

4 You immediately come to a gate and ladder-stile. Cross them and continue ahead. *Soon stunning views over the Dyfi estuary open up to the south. A slate slab on the right marks 'Carn March Arthur'. Here you will see an indentation in the rock, in legend said to be the hoof-print of Arthur's horse. One tale says it was left when Arthur and his horse leapt across the Dyfi when pursued by his enemies, but the observant (and cynical) will not be satisfied with the alignment. Another tale says it was left by Arthur's horse after he had dragged a monster from Llyn Barfog. Or maybe it was left by Huw Gadarn, otherwise known as 'Huw the Mighty', who captured a monster and dragged it into the lake. You can take your pick. Huw Gadarn is thought to have originated from Defrobane, which is now Istanbul, about 1800BC. He is said to have mnemonically systematised the learnings of Druids, who he led west. He claimed great intellectual powers, and is also reputed to be responsible for the founding of Stonehenge, the introduction of glass-making and Ogham script. He established that the 'Gorsedd', or assembly of Druids and Bards, should be held in an open grassy space, in full view of the people.* Continue along the track, crossing the next gate and stile. Soon the track starts to descend.

5 You reach two gates by a house. Take the LEFT-hand gate, following the direction indicated by the sign. After 10 yards go through a second gate, then immediately turn half-RIGHT, following the direction indicated by the sign. Cross the stile in the fence and continue downhill, veering slightly RIGHT to a waymark post. Continue downhill, Bearing slightly RIGHT to come to waymarks on a post by a gate.

6 DO NOT go through the gate, but just continue downhill leaving the gate to your left and walking to the stile ahead. Cross the stile and turn RIGHT to walk across the field. Cross a second stile, step across a tiny stream and cross the ladder stile ahead to rejoin your outward path. Turn LEFT to return to the car park.

WALK 4
DOWN BY THE DYFI

DESCRIPTION The initial part of this 2½-mile walk traverses the flood plain of the River Dyfi, the haunt of wildfowl and duck. A short section beside the river leads to the return through woods and over gentle hills. Try to make time for a visit to the church in Pennal. Allow 2 hours.

START Behind the church at Pennal. SH 699004.

DIRECTIONS From the Clock Tower in Machynlleth, take the A487 north to cross the Dyfi Bridge and turn left onto the A493 towards Aberdyfi. After 3 miles you reach Pennal. Park behind the church. Bus 29 from Machynlleth to Pennal operates Mon–Sat.

1 Walk to the main road by the church, and turn RIGHT. Cross the bridge, cross the road and walk along to a gate, with a footpath sign, on your LEFT. Go through the gate, and walk with a stream on your LEFT. Go through the next gate and veer to the RIGHT along a track, ignoring the ford.

2 Cross a wide concrete bridge and turn RIGHT to go through a gate. Turn LEFT and walk across the field to another drainage ditch. Walk with this ditch on your RIGHT. You reach a gate and ladder stile. Go through and continue ahead.

3 When you reach a footbridge on your right, cross it and turn LEFT. After about 20 yards look for a ditch to your RIGHT. Walk beside this ditch. Eventually you climb a small embankment to reach the River Dyfi. *This is Llyn Bwtri pool, where craft making their way up river to Derwenlas could ride out low water.* Turn RIGHT, to walk with the river on your LEFT.

4 After a few yards you cross a very rudimentary fence stile, and then continue along the embankment. Ignore a stile down to your right, and continue until you reach a

footbridge on your RIGHT. *A short distance to the south-east is the railway bridge over the Dyfi. This was officially opened on 14 August 1867. The first engine to cross the river under its own power was the Oswestry & Newtown's Volunteer, which had been transported from Ynyslas to Aberdyfi by barge, to return over the bridge on 30 July 1866, driven by John Ward. When built, the bridge had a 35 ft-wide opening section, which was drawn back under the superstructure to allow the passage of boats. It was finally permanently fixed in 1914. Dovey Junction Station, a lonely outpost, presented an entirely bleak prospect when first opened, with no shelter at all on the solitary platform.* Cross the footbridge and walk with a drainage ditch to your LEFT.

5 Go through the first gate on your LEFT, crossing the ditch, and walk half-RIGHT to *Ynys* farm. When you reach the farm, walk to the RIGHT to join the tarmac lane, and follow that uphill and away from the buildings. Continue along the lane.

6 As you come to *Penmaen Bach*, and before the lane curves to the right, go through a gate on the RIGHT-hand side, and walk straight ahead over some exposed rocky ground and between trees, to the low summit ahead. Continue towards the left-hand side of the buildings ahead. When you reach the fence on your RIGHT, go through the gate and walk to the buildings, passing the *Open Door Team Development* buildings on your right. Follow the lane between the buildings and on to a gate.

7 Go through the gate and walk initially AHEAD, then to the LEFT around the hill to come to a gate. Climb or go through the gate and follow the path with a fence to the right, and trees to the left. Cross the next stile and continue with a fence to the right to another stile. Cross this and follow the path gently downhill through trees. When the path joins a track (with leap-frog posts to the right), turn LEFT and continue downhill.

8 As you reach the holiday bungalows at Plas Talgarth continue straight ahead, to eventually join the road out of the holiday park. Turn LEFT and walk along the access road. Just after the road crosses a stream, turn RIGHT to cross the fence stile. Walk to the right of the tree-covered mound, then veer left to reach the main road. *To the left of the path, as you approach the main road, is the Tomen Las, a prominent tree covered mound. It was from here that Owain Glyndwr is said to have sent the 'Pennal Letter', in 1406, at a time when Europe had two Popes, one in Rome, and one in Avignon in France. Glyndwr's letter stated that the Welsh would support Benedict XIII, the French Pope, following certain conditions.* Go through the gate and turn RIGHT to return to Pennal.

*T**ry to make time** to visit the church of St Peter ad Vincula, one of only five such churches in Britain with that dedication. A church was founded on this site in the 6thC*

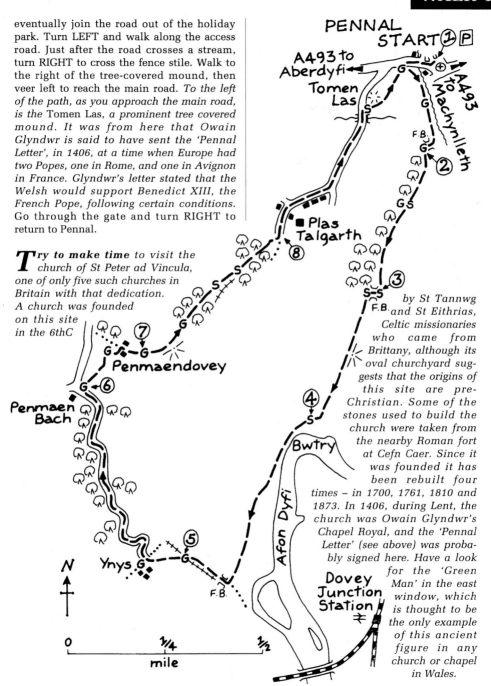

by St Tannwg and St Eithrias, Celtic missionaries who came from Brittany, although its oval churchyard suggests that the origins of this site are pre-Christian. Some of the stones used to build the church were taken from the nearby Roman fort at Cefn Caer. Since it was founded it has been rebuilt four times – in 1700, 1761, 1810 and 1873. In 1406, during Lent, the church was Owain Glyndwr's Chapel Royal, and the 'Pennal Letter' (see above) was probably signed here. Have a look for the 'Green Man' in the east window, which is thought to be the only example of this ancient figure in any church or chapel in Wales.

9

WALK 5
WOODLAND WANDERS ABOVE PENNAL

DESCRIPTION A 7-mile walk amidst the woodlands in the hills behind Pennal. Narrow valleys, ancient green tracks and the occasional sweeping view combine to make this a memorable walk. A ford on this route could be a little deep during *wet* weather, so please bear this in mind. Allow 4 hours. **START** Behind the church at Pennal.

SH 699004.
DIRECTIONS From the Clock Tower in Machynlleth, take the A487 north to cross the Dyfi Bridge and turn left onto the A493 towards Aberdyfi. After 3 miles you reach Pennal. Park behind the church. Bus 29 from Machynlleth to Pennal operates Mon-Sat.

1 From the church, walk away from the main road, turn RIGHT at the junction and walk through Felindre and continue gently uphill. When the road forks (by a seat), head to the RIGHT and continue. Bear LEFT at the next fork (signed 'Cycleway 8') and continue, crossing the bridge over the Afon Pennal. Eventually the road reaches *Ffarm Gyllellog*.

2 Go through the gate, cross the farmyard, go through a second gate and continue to a third gate. Go through, and enter the forest. Continue along the track to a junction. Remember this junction, as you will turn here on the return route

3 Walk to the RIGHT, along the forestry road, which then gently curves to the left, with a stream down on the right.

4 At a footpath sign, just beyond a house away across the valley, veer half-RIGHT downhill towards the stream, where you cross a bridge and turn LEFT.

Soon you join a forest road, where you turn LEFT. After 40 yards fork half-RIGHT up a fine mossy green path through the trees. A path joins from the right, but continue ahead. The path climbs quite steeply. Eventually you emerge at a 'T' junction of forest roads.

5 Turn LEFT along the forest road and continue until the road makes a wide hairpin left. Here you will see a waymarked grassy track AHEAD. Follow this into the forest. The track soon traverses a muddy patch where a stream crosses. Veer LEFT here. The path begins to descend and soon joins a forest road, where you head to the RIGHT.

6 At the next junction (by forestry sign 'RO905') continue to the RIGHT for a few yards. Opposite a vehicle 'No Entry' sign turn sharp LEFT up a grassy track to a gate. Go through and head to the right up the field to a waymark post, which directs you to the right, with a Leylandii hedge on your left. You join a

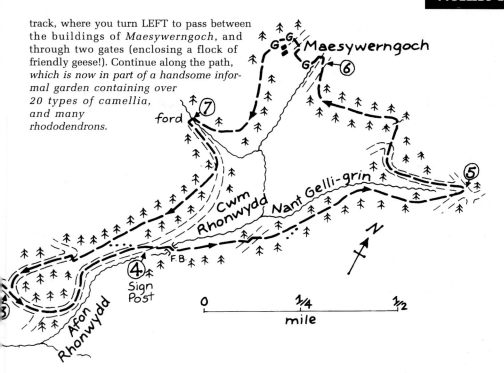

track, where you turn LEFT to pass between the buildings of *Maesywerngoch*, and through two gates (enclosing a flock of friendly geese!). Continue along the path, *which is now in part of a handsome informal garden containing over 20 types of camellia, and many rhododendrons.*

7 The path eventually descends to a ford, which you cross. Turn LEFT and walk along the forestry road for about 100 yards until you see a signed footpath heading into the trees on the RIGHT. Follow this path, *although tree felling operations may require a minor diversion here. If so, just stay on the forestry road until you reach a footpath signpost (which you passed on the outward route), where you fork right up a track into the trees to rejoin the path.* Continue along

the track until you reach a felled area, just beyond a point where power lines cross overhead. Turn sharp RIGHT and walk 35 yards uphill to reach a forestry road. Turn LEFT here and continue along the road, which curves to the left. Look out for the junction with the track you came along at point **3**. Turn RIGHT here to walk back through the farmyard and along the road to Pennal.

11

WALK 6
BEACH AND BOG AT BORTH

DESCRIPTION This full walk covers 5½ miles of a level route which encompasses the edge of Borth Bog and a fine stroll back along the sea front. It is easily reduced to a little over 3½ miles by making a shorter return walk. If you are unhappy about making the unprotected crossing of the railway bridge at Ynyslas, you can just walk the Borth section. Whichever option you choose, you will find this an easy level route with extensive views of the surrounding hills and, on a clear day, the full sweep of Cardigan Bay. Allow 3 hours for the full walk.

START The car park on the golf course at Ynyslas for the walk including the railway bridge, *or roadside at the northern end of*

Borth for the shorter walk which avoids the railway bridge. SN 606925.

DIRECTIONS From the Clock Tower in Machynlleth, take the A487 south towards Aberystwyth. After about 8½ miles, at Tre'r-ddol, turn right onto the B4353 and follow this until you join the coast road at a 'T' junction. Opposite is the entrance to a car park (modest charge in season). Drive in and park. *If you do not want to cross the railway bridge on your walk,* turn left and drive towards Borth. Park at the roadside, near the station. You can take the train from Machynlleth to Borth, or bus 2 to Rhydypennau, then 511 or 512 to Ynyslas (Mon-Sat).

1 *These are directions for the full walk.* From the car park, walk with the sea to your left, and look out for an old red-brick look-out post on a small hill. *Ynyslas dunes were used as an artillery testing range during World War II. The great gun known as 'Big Bertha' was brought down from Scotland for testing here.*

2 Walk along the track directly opposite, go through a gateway and continue ahead. Go through another two gates to emerge on a concrete track, where a lane joins from the right. Continue ahead towards the boatyard. Cross a cattle grid and join the road.

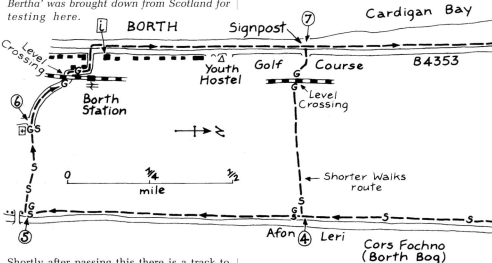

Shortly after passing this there is a track to the right, with an old brick building beside. Turn RIGHT along this track and *carefully* cross the golf course. Go through a gateway and cross the road.

Continue ahead over the bridge, looking out for a footpath sign on the right, behind a low crash barrier.

3 Turn RIGHT at the sign to walk with the Afon Leri to your right, soon crossing a rough fence stile. Continue ahead. *You now have to cross the railway, and the railway bridge over the river. Listen carefully for trains. If you can hear a train, wait until it has passed. If you have young children with you, make sure they are under control, and make sure they stay with you. Do not linger on the bridge.* CROSS WITH EXTREME CARE. A gate gives access to the railway: go through the gate, cross the track, turn right and cross the bridge. Once off the bridge, turn left and cross the stile to continue with the river now on your left. Cross two more stiles (there may be no fence by the second). *On the other side of the Afon Leri is Cors Fochno (Borth Bog), renowned for its wild flowers, moths and adder population. Otters have also been seen.*

4 You come to a gate and a stile where a track joins from the right. Cross the stile and walk with the river to your left.

5 You reach another gate and stile: cross and immediately turn RIGHT, walking with a small hill and waterworks to your left. Continue ahead, crossing the next two stiles (keeping a rough hedge to your left). *This is the 'Uppingham Path', and you will notice two inscribed slate seats on the left, recording Uppingham School and the years 1876 and 1877. Borth's reputation as a health giving resort had spread across England, and its restorative qualities were noted by the Reverend Thring of Uppingham in Rutland, whose village was suffering an epidemic. He evacuated the entire school to Borth, where the school built a friendly and lasting relationship with the village. As well as the seats, the boys left a stained glass window and a lectern in the church.* Finally you cross a gate and stile to join the road below St Matthew's Church.

6 Turn RIGHT along the lane. At the level crossing *ensure that no trains are coming*, go through the gate, cross the track and turn RIGHT. Go through a gate and then turn LEFT by the station to emerge at the seafront. Turn RIGHT.

7 Now walk along the beach, sea wall or road, with the sea to your left. *If you are taking a shortened route, avoiding the unprotected railway crossing, look out for the signposted footpath on the right which crosses the golf course, and the railway (through two gates), to join the walk at point **4**. Before the last ice age, the coastline was over 7 miles further to the west, and this land was covered with Scots pine, alder and birch. Stories of the land once extending seawards are clearly founded in truth (see Walk **1**), since tree stumps are uncovered during low spring tides.* Continue ahead to return to the car park

A story tells of Maelgwyn, a local chieftain, who decided to resolve a rulership dispute by having his rivals, and himself, sit in chairs on the beach while the tide came in. The last to remain would become king. Maelgwyn built his chair of waxed feathers, and floated while his rivals submerged one by one. He became king: perhaps, for his guile, deservedly so. This ceremony is still celebrated here.

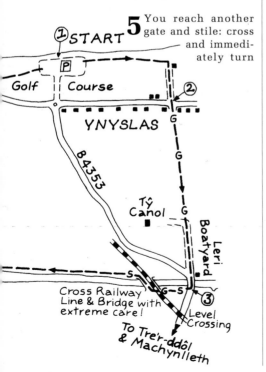

WALK 7
A STROLL ABOVE TRE'R-DDOL

DESCRIPTION A delightful 4-mile walk from the Wildfowler pub, on quiet farm roads which initially climb through woodlands to give expansive views across the Dyfi towards Aberdyfi. The road then passes along a quiet valley towards the old Bryndyfi mine, before descending back to Tre'r-ddol through farms and forestry. Allow 2½ hours. **START** The Wildfowler pub in Tre'r-ddol.

SN 659923.

DIRECTIONS From the Clock Tower in Machynlleth, take the A487 south towards Aberystwyth. After about 8½ miles, fork left into Tre'r-ddol and park at the roadside by the Wildfowler pub. Or you can take bus 2 (or 514, but check) from Machynlleth (Mon-Sat).

1 From the pub, walk towards the church, turning LEFT up the lane before the bridge. Continue along this lane, which climbs steeply uphill through woodland, and turns sharply right to pass through a gateway by *Llety-lwydin*. When the road reaches a T junction, turn LEFT.

2 Go through a gateway and continue. *When the road makes a very sharp left turn, you can continue ahead along the unsurfaced lane. Through the second gate on the right a track leads to the extensive remains of the Bryndyfi Lead Mine. After sinking trial levels,*

14

work began here in earnest in 1881. The mine was designed by D C Davies & Son, and initially employed 100 men. Extensive developments at the surface have left well executed buddle circles (a buddle separated the crushed ore from gangue, or ore matrix), wheelpits, ore bins and a crusher house in a remarkably good state of repair. Deposits of ore, however, did not live up to initial expectations, and the mine closed after only a couple of years, having brought just 24 tons of lead ore to the surface. A tramway connected these workings with others about half-a-mile to the north-east.

3 Follow the lane sharply to the left, and begin gradually to descend. Pass through three gates at *Cefn gweirog*, and another at *Ynystudor*, and continue until the road enters forestry and starts to descend, and a track crosses. Turn LEFT here and walk along the forest road. Ignore tracks off to the left and continue ahead. Gradually the forest road becomes less distinct – look out for a clear woodland path on the right, and maintain your direction along this. It descends to a gate. Go through and turn LEFT to return to the Wildfowler pub.

*Y***r Hen Capel Museum**, *in Tre'r ddol, is worth visiting. This museum depicts 19thC religious life in Wales, and is housed in a handsome former Wesleyan chapel linked with the origins of the 1859 religious revival, which had such a momentous effect on the social life of rural, and industrial, Wales. It is usually open 10.00-17.00 Mon-Sat from April-September (closed Sun).*

Yr Hen Capel

Ynys-hir was purchased by the RSPB in 1969, and has subsequently been enlarged to cover 1056 acres. It is a site of great importance, encompassing several Sites of Special Scientific Interest (SSSI). The chosen route of this walk encompasses the whole variety of habitats available here. The initial part, to the east of the railway line, takes in saltmarsh, peatland and the freshwater pools and ditches by Marian Mawr, a rush dominated field. Returning to the southwest of the Information Centre the walk continues through mixed woodlands, parts of which date from the 17thC and were cut for use as charcoal in the lead and iron smelting industries (see Dyfi Furnace, below). Low-lying peatland and coniferous woods are passed at Covert Du, with further saltmarsh by the Breakwater Hide. Your return skirts Ynys Edwin, where the remnants of peat bogs remain amidst land drained by the farmer.

Freshwater pools and ditches have been created at Ynys Edwin, Covert Du, Covert Coch

and West Marsh, and livestock grazing maintains the saltings for wildfowl in winter. Much of the oak-wood is now fenced to allow seedlings to regenerate, and many indigenous woodland plants have been replanted. The most important of the habitats at Ynys-hir are the saltmarshes, where important populations of as many as 3000 wigeon, and a modest 100 or so Greenland white-fronted geese may be seen in winter. There are also mallard, teal, shelduck, pintail, red-breasted merganiser and goldeneye. Curlews are present throughout the year. Many characteristic woodland species are found in the oak-woods, along with lesser spotted woodpeckers and nuthatches. A few reed warblers may be seen in Covert Du, and there is a heronry in the wood on Domen Las. The characteristic local birds of prey: red kites, hen harriers, merlins and peregrines can be seen all year.

Come in May to see carpets of bluebells and wood anemones, or later to enjoy foxgloves and flowering cow-wheat.

Saltings Hide ②
G-S
F.B.

⑦

③ R.S.P.
P
① STAR

Ynys Edwin

F.B. ⑥

Breakwater Hide ⑤
F.B.
Ynys Eidiol Hide
Covert Du Hide
F.B.
F.B.

Ynyshir Hide

Ynys-hir Farm

④

N

0   1/4   1/2
mile

Aberystwyth A487 to

Walk 8
THE ESTUARY AT YNYS-HIR

1 Take the path towards the rear of the reception building, and go through the gate. Turn RIGHT and continue along the wide path, continuing ahead at a path junction. Go through a gate and cross the railway bridge, then turn LEFT through the small left-hand gate (you will return through the larger gate to the right). Follow the path then soon bear LEFT to walk with a fence on your left. Cross a small footbridge and reach Saltings Hide.

2 Continue on the path, passing the hide. Go through a gate and turn RIGHT. The path borders the edge of the saltmarsh for a short distance, then crosses a stile to head inland. Follow it to reach the bridge over the railway, crossed earlier. Go over the bridge and continue to a paths junction, where you turn RIGHT.

3 Turn LEFT through a gate into woods, and follow the path. When the path forks by a 'Reception 400m' sign, go LEFT. The path climbs a wooded hill and passes Ynys-hir hide. Continue, and at the next paths junction, turn LEFT for Ynys Eidiol & Breakwater Hides.

4 You reach gates either side of a track. Go through, cross the track and continue ahead along the path, which curves to the right and crosses a substantial footbridge, and then a second smaller footbridge, where the path turns left. Pass Covert Du Hide, cross a small footbridge and follow the path to the right. Pass Ynys Eidiol Hide and cross another small footbridge.

5 The path reaches a gate onto a track. Go through the gate, cross to the stile opposite, climb over and continue to Breakwater Hide. Follow the path around to the right, cross a stile and continue

DESCRIPTION An easy 4-mile walk around the RSPB Reserve at Ynys-hir. Initially amidst woods, the walk soon extends into the saltmarsh of the estuary, with excellent views up and down river. There is, of course, excellent bird-life. If you are already an RSPB member, access is free. If you are not, the charge is £2 50 for individuals, and 50p for children (concession £1.50). It represents good value, and the walk is worth doing at any time of year. Allow 2½ hours.
START From the car park at Ynys-hir RSPB Reserve. SN 682964.
DIRECTIONS From the Clock Tower in Machynlleth, take the A487 south towards Aberystwyth. After about 6 miles, at Eglwys fach, turn right into the RSPB Reserve and park below the Information Centre. The reserve is open 09.00–21.00, or sunset if earlier. You can take bus 2 (or 514, but check) to Furnace, from Machynlleth (Mon-Sat).

beside the railway.

6 The path parts company with the railway by turning RIGHT over a footbridge. Cross the stile ahead and continue, keeping by the left-hand fence. The path bends to the left over a small brow, and forks. Take the LEFT fork through a gate, and continue, following the path. As the path bends to the right you pass through two more gates. Continue along the track.

7 Just beyond a small rocky outcrop to your left, a track joins from the right. Veer LEFT to continue along the track. Soon you rejoin your outward path. Turn RIGHT to return to the RSPB Information Centre.

If you have time, it is worth visiting the Dyfi Furnace, which is just a short distance along the A487 towards Aberystwyth, on the left. It was built around 1755, and is open 09.30-18.30 daily from Easter to late October. Entry is free.

1 From the Black Lion, walk in the Aberystwyth direction, turning sharp LEFT uphill along a signposted footpath by *Brynderwen*. The path zig-zags uphill through woods, passes through a gate and continues, to join a track. Turn RIGHT and walk for a short distance to a path which climbs sharp LEFT up the hillside (if you reach the signposts on the main track, you have passed it!).

2 When the path joins a narrow road, continue ahead. When the road bends to the left through a gate, continue AHEAD along the green track (the two apparent routes become one just over the brow).

3 You come to a fence with a gate and stile missing (these have been requested). Carefully climb the fence and continue, veering slightly right to a gate. Go through the gate and then veer slightly left downhill. *The original course of the bridleway can be discerned in many places along here, with shallow cuttings through rock being the most obvious clue. Follow this old trackway as closely as you can.* Go through another gate and continue, veering slightly left away from the trees to reach a gate by a small rock outcrop. Go through and zig-zag downhill to join a track by the river. Turn LEFT.

4 Go through a gate and continue on ahead. *This is Cwm Llyfnant, a very pretty valley, with tall rocky cliffs to the left, and the tumbling Llyfnant to the right, all en-closed by trees. It has been designated as an SSSI, and most of the 195 acre site is owned by the RSPB. The middle section has the remnants*

of ancient woodland, with cliffs and scree on the south side containing huge boulders rich with ferns and mosses, thriving in the humid oceanic conditions found here. Woods of sessile oak and mountain ash rise from a shrub layer of hazel. Amongst the flora is a sub-species of wood

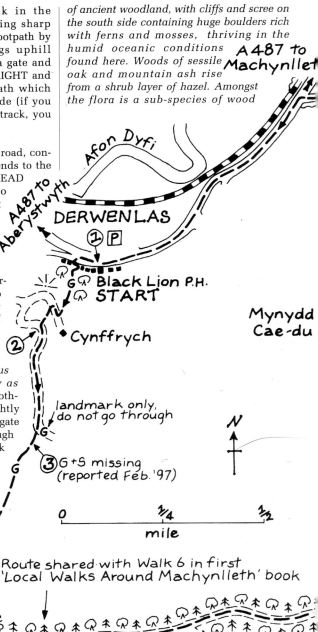

A487 to Machynlleth

Afon Dyfi

A487 to Aberystwyth

DERWENLAS ① P

G Black Lion P.H. START

Cynffrych

Mynydd Cae-du

landmark only, do not go through

③ G+S missing (reported Feb. '97)

N

0   ¼   ½
              mile

Route shared with Walk 6 in first 'Local Walks Around Machynlleth' book

Old Mine

④ Old Mine   Cwm Llyfnant

18

stitchwort in its only known location in Ceredigion. A small cave close to the summit contains luminous moss, and the summit is rich with bilberry and broad buckler-fern. At the level of the river there is an old tunnel entrance to the left, and another very short tunnel a little further along on the right. These were exploratory mine workings only, with no evidence of production. Stay on the main track, ignoring branches off to the right. You gradually climb away from the river.

Mynydd Garth Gwynion

5 You leave the woods through a gate. Turn LEFT to follow a rough track, with a stone wall on your right. Cross a gate and continue. Go through the next gate and walk downhill to join the road.

6 Now walk ahead along this quiet road until it joins the main road. Turn LEFT to return to the start at Derwenlas.

Derwenlas ('green oak') used to be, as the highest navigable point on the river, the port for Machynlleth. Indeed one of the riverside fields was called 'Cae Wharf', the field of the wharf, and there were three quays: Tafan Isa, Quay Ellis and Quay Ward. 40,000 ft of timber, 15,000 oak poles, 500 tons of bark, 1500 tons of slate and 586 tons of lead were exported in 1847. It was served by 'flats' and sloops, and shipbuilding was carried on here until 1869 when the last craft, the

WALK 9
DERWENLAS AND CWM LLYFNANT

DESCRIPTION A 4½ mile walk where superb views over the Dyfi Valley are soon replaced by the intimacy of the beautiful Cwm Llyfnant. The return is along a quiet minor road beside the Nant Rhisglog. There is one stile missing on this route, so a fence has to be carefully climbed (point **3**). Allow 3 hours.

START From the Black Lion pub at Derwenlas. SN 721991.

DIRECTIONS From the Clock Tower in Machynlleth, take the A487 south towards Aberystwyth. The first village on this road is Derwenlas, 2 miles from the town. Park on the left, by the Black Lion. Or you can take bus 2 from Machynlleth (Mon-Sat).

'Rebecca', was launched. The wharves were isolated when the course of the Dyfi was diverted away from the village when the railway track was laid, and they soon silted up, although the wharf downstream at Morben continued trading for a while. Indeed it was the building of the railway which brought the last glorious flush of trade to the river. Derwenlas was also served by the Corris Tramway (currently undergoing restoration at the Corris end), which was originally worked by gravity above Machynlleth, and horse drawn below. Later, steam locomotives were used. There were, at one time, plans for the railway junction now sited downstream at Dovey Junction to be positioned here: it would have been less exposed to storm and flood; the bridge over the Dyfi would have been cheaper to build; and it would have given a rail connection to Pennal, on the northern side.

The Black Lion pub at Derwenlas, a handsome and cosy place some 450 years old, at one time stood beside the old Machynlleth to Aberystwyth turnpike road, and also served the quays.

WALK 10
A TASTE OF GLYNDWR

DESCRIPTION Splendid views of the Dyfi Valley feature strongly on this 5 mile walk which, for a good part of the route, shares its course with Glyndwr's Way. All the paths are clear and wide, although one short stretch can be muddy. Allow 3 hours.
START From Commins Coch. SH 035846.
DIRECTIONS From the Clock Tower in Machynlleth, take the A489 east towards Newtown. At the roundabout at Cemmaes Road, take the A470 straight ahead. At Commins Coch, immediately after the road crosses the bridge over the river, turn sharp left to go under the railway. About ¼ mile up the lane, park in the lay-by opposite a grey corrugated iron shed. You can take bus 522 from Machynlleth to Commins Coch (not Sundays), and there is a post-bus service.

1 From the lay-by, continue along the lane, forking LEFT along the signed bridle-path (also to Glyntwymyn). Continue along the track, passing through two gates.

another gate. *There are good views from here, and soon the windfarm on Mynydd y Cemmaes*

2 Go through a small gate off the track, to walk along the top edge of a field, avoiding the house. Rejoin the track through a second gate, then pass through two more gates to continue along the track. Pass through the next gate and continue, ignoring a track which forks off to the right. Carry on downhill.

3 When the track joins a signed bridleway, turn RIGHT. *You are now on Glyndwr's Way (see below).* When a signed green track branches off to the LEFT, follow this. At a track crossing, continue ahead, up to a gate. Go through, then walk ahead, uphill, to

20

(Walk 11) comes into view. Go through this gate and, maintaining your direction, reach another gate, tucked into the field corner.

4 Go through this gate, and continue downhill along a track to another gate. Go through, cross a tiny stream and follow the track to the left of a farmhouse. Go through the next gate and, as you leave the farm, turn right through a signed gate. The track turns to the right and continues, passing through six gates, curving first left and then right. *There are superb and expansive views from this section over the Dyfi Valley.* Eventually you reach a lane, close to *Gwalia*.

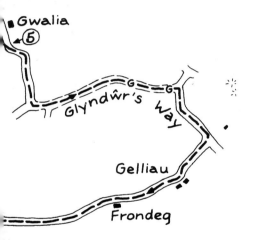

5 Maintain your direction along the lane until it turns sharply right, with a track to the left. Turn LEFT, going gently uphill along this often muddy track. Pass through two gates to emerge at a road. Turn RIGHT. At the next road junction, turn RIGHT again, leave Glyndwr's Way, and return to the start.

So **who was Glyndwr?** *In 1284 Edward I completed England's conquest of Wales, when Llywelyn was killed in a skirmish with English forces at Climery, near Builth Wells. Owain ap Gruffydd (Owain Glyndwr) was born around 1359, the son of Gryffydd Fychan and descendant of the royal house of Powys. He probably served as an apprentice in law in London, staying at the Inns of Court. Later he became Squire to Henry*

Bolingbroke, King Richard's cousin, and during this period he would have learned his fighting skills, which he probably honed during campaigns in Scotland and Europe.
In 1398, his military career over, he settled near Sycharth in a moated wooden house, married to Margaret Hanmer and with a 'nest of children'.
In 1400 there was discontent in Wales and Scotland and, on 16 September, Owain was proclaimed Prince of Wales, encouraged by Welsh hatred for the English King and his Marcher Lords. On the 18th September Owain's motley army rode into Ruthin. By the 24th they had raided other towns and were closing upon Welshpool when they were routed near Shrewsbury. Henry VI's army arrived the next day, and subsequently subdued the rebellion. All the rebels, except Owain, were pardoned, but the Welsh as a whole were badly treated by the English parliament.
Rebellion re-occurred in 1401, with Conwy Castle being burned. Owain raised an army, and Henry responded, strengthening garrisons and reinforcing castles. A comet which appeared in the sky in 1402 was taken as an omen, since its tail was said to point towards Wales. Owain's rebellion grew, defeating the English at Pilleth, near Knighton, at a place called Bryn Glas. Owain then moved south, and also blockaded the castles at Harlech and Caernarfon.
By 1404 Owain had secured Wales, taken Harlech Castle and established a Parliament in Machynlleth. He tried to make an alliance with the French, but this came to nothing, although he tried again, calling a Parliament in Machynlleth and sending the Pennal Letter (See Walk 4).
Eventually King Henry became ill, and gave Prince Henry a free hand to campaign, successfully, in Wales, turning Owain into a fugitive. In 1407 the rebellion faded through starvation and a lack of funds, and Aberystwyth and Harlech Castles, held by Glyndwr, were under siege. By 1409 both had fallen. In 1410 it was all over.
Owain Glyndwr faded from history, and was thought to have died on the 20th September 1415 at Monnington-on-Wye, or, perhaps, on an exposed mountain ridge in Gwynedd.

WALK 11
FARMING THE WIND

DESCRIPTION Choose a clear day for this 5½ mile walk if you can, when the effort involved in climbing Mynydd y Cemmaes and negotiating the boggy ground will be amply repaid with stunning views along the Dyfi Valley, as far as Aberdyfi and out to sea. You will also get a close look at the Cemmaes Wind Farm. The route is not too difficult to follow, but it is wet and boggy in two or three places. Allow 3½ hours.

START The lay-by opposite the caravan park at Cwm Llinau. SH 854083.

DIRECTIONS From the Clock Tower in Machynlleth, take the A489 east towards Newtown. At the roundabout at Cemmaes Road, turn left onto the A470, and continue through Cemmaes to Cwm Llinau. Turn RIGHT here and after about ½ mile, park in the rough lay-by opposite the caravan park. Or you can take bus 518 to Cwm Llinau, and walk up from the village.

1 Walk up the lane, passing the entrance to the caravan park on your left. Where the road forks, go LEFT downhill. Continue, going through a gate. When the track forks, carry on ahead to the next gate. Go through and continue along the now pleasantly grassy track, with a stone wall to your right. *It is worth stopping for a rest, and looking back to enjoy the view.*

2 When the stone wall ends, go through an old gate on your RIGHT, and walk diagonally across rough ground towards a stream. Continue with the stream tumbling down on your right, negotiating the rough ground as best you can. When you draw level with trees on your right, go through the remains of a gate and continue alongside the stream (which you can cross at any point where conditions seem suitable).

3 You reach a gate into the forestry plantation. Go through, and walk ahead as waymarked. Continue ahead and slightly right as waymarked at the next junction, and reach a gate. Go through, turn RIGHT and walk towards the wind farm, with the fence over to the right. The ground is wet and boggy in places here.

4 When you reach a gate, go through and walk between the two aero-generators ahead, to meet a track. Turn LEFT. *The view from here towards Aberdyfi and the mountains of Cadair Idris, on a clear day, is quite stunning. It is worth stopping for a while to enjoy it.* Continue along the service track through the wind farm. *The twenty-four twin-bladed aero-generators look very large when seen from close-up. When they are turning energetically, they produce 300 kw/hour. The blades began spinning late 1992, and the wind farm was officially opened by the Secretary of State for Wales in early 1993. Twin blades seem to be quite unusual now, with three bladed towers presently seeming to be more common.*

5 Go through a gateway on the track and veer half-RIGHT away from the track over rough grassland, to reach a boggy patch with a fence just beyond the head of a cwm

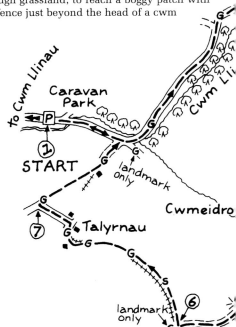

(valley). Pick your way across the wet ground and join a good wide track which goes steeply downhill. Go through a gate and continue. *Again the view ahead is splendid. The track becomes 'green'.*

6 You reach another gate. DO NOT go through, but turn RIGHT to walk downhill, with the hedge to your left. Cross a stile and continue to a gate. Go through this and carry on with the hedge now to your right. Go through the next gate and continue,

ignoring the first gate to your right. Continue to a gate down to your right, and go through. Walk along the road, and follow it as it turns left.

7 When the road turns left again, turn RIGHT to go through a gate and walk across a field, with a fence to your right, towards a house. Join a lane by the house and continue ahead through a gate. Walk along the lane to the road, where you turn LEFT to return to the start.

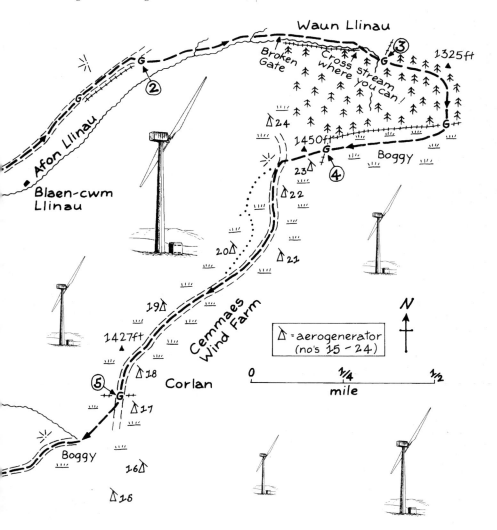

WALK 12
THE THREE PEAKS VIEW

DESCRIPTION A fine 4½ mile walk in the hilly country to the east of Machynlleth. Starting from the church at Darowen, the walk passes a splendid standing stone and a handsomely converted mill before climbing to the summit of Fron Goch, a modest enough hill but one with exceptional views. Allow 3 hours.

START From the parking area by the church in Darowen. SH 830018.

DIRECTIONS From the Clock Tower in Machynlleth, take the A489 east towards Newtown. After passing through Penegoes, take the next turning on the right, signposted to Darowen. Pass through Abercegir, then fork left steeply uphill to Darowen. Park on the village green, opposite the church. There is a post-bus service from Machynlleth.

1 From the village green, walk down the lane opposite the church, behind the old school buildings. When the tarmac ends at *Tan-llan* farm, continue down the lane, which can get very wet after rain. Cross the first stream and continue to the second, which is crossed by footbridge. The track climbs to reach a cross-tracks, at the entrance to *Pwlliwrch* farm. Continue straight ahead. *Just before the track starts to drop down towards Tal-y-Wern, before a lane leaves to the left, look over the gate on the right to see the standing stone 'Maen llwyd'. This stone is one of three which were thought to mark a 'noddfa', or sanctuary. Those suspected of wrong-doing were given a head start to reach the area enclosed by the stones and, if successful, were allowed to go free. The stone here, the largest of the two surviving, stands in a field known as Cae yr hen eglwys (old church field). A ley-line through the surviving stones links these with the church. The third stone, Carreg y Noddfa, once stood to the east of Cwm Bychan Mawr, but was broken for building stone around 1860. There is no right of way into the field.*

2 When you come to a T junction at the entrance to *Rhosdyrnog*, turn RIGHT and walk down to the road, where you turn LEFT. At the village of Tal-y-Wern, turn RIGHT downhill, following the sign for Melinbyrhedyn. The road climbs steeply, and twists and turns. Soon you reach a track on your right, marked by a *Llwybr Cyhoeddus* sign. Turn RIGHT through the gate and follow the track, which enters trees and soon accompanies a stream to the right. Walk through trees to emerge at a field opposite a handsome converted mill. Walk diagonally LEFT up the field to a converted farmhouse.

3 Climb the gate below the house, and walk down the lane at the front of the house. Go through the gate at the bottom of the lane, and turn LEFT to walk along the road.

4 Shortly before the road bends away to the right, take the way-marked grassy track half-RIGHT uphill. Continue, crossing the road and maintaining your direction uphill. Go through a gate and then immediately leave the track to walk half-RIGHT up the field, to a gate in a field corner. Go through the gate and turn LEFT. Walk to a gateway, go through and turn RIGHT, to walk with a hedge on your right.

Bryn llwyn

⑤

5 Cross the stile tucked away in the field corner and immediately turn RIGHT to walk steeply uphill, with a fence on your right. Continue until you reach a gate on your right. DO NOT go through the gate, but walk to the LEFT up the green track opposite. When you reach another gate, DO NOT go through, but turn RIGHT to walk uphill, using the concessionary path. Continue to the top of Fron Goch. *The summit here is a mere 930 ft high,*

To Aberceg & Machynlle

N

0   ½

mile

enclosed by the feint remains of the ditch and wall of a Romano-British hill fort, yet it offers stunning views. On a clear day you will see the sea at Aberdyfi, and the summits of Cadair Idris, Aran Fawddwy and Plynlimon Fawr. Walk downhill, with the village of Darowen ahead and to the right.

6 Cross the stile beside a gate, turn sharply LEFT and walk downhill to another stile. Cross this and turn RIGHT to rejoin the right of way. Walk with a hedge on your right. Go through a gate and follow the track to a stile. You are now passing Bryn Crogwr, 'Hangman's Hill'. The tree used for hangings once stood by the barns over on your left. It was felled around 1900. Cross the stile and maintain your direction downhill, joining a fence to the right. Go through two gateways and turn RIGHT, to walk with a large grey shed to the left.

Go through two gates to join the road in Darowen. Turn LEFT to return to the start.

Darowen stands at a height of around 600ft, yet commands a splendid view over the foothills of the Plynlimons. The church is built on a raised circular site, giving a clue to its antiquity, and this, combined with the accompanying standing stones, suggests

that the village may have been of considerable importance at the time of the Wessex Culture, around 2000 BC. The church of St Tudur was founded in the 7thC, and it is claimed that the saint is buried here. His feast day, on the 15th October, used to be celebrated by a young man being carried around the parish on his companions shoulders. The present building dates from 1864, and replaced a 14thC building which was falling down. The new church cost £667. 0.9½p to build. There is still a weekly service, conducted in Welsh, at 14.00 each Sunday. The Methodist chapel was founded in 1823, and was used regularly until December 1987.

The school, now used as both a residence and a glass workshop, was opened in 1841, and extended in 1871. It finally closed in 1971. The 18thC saw the heyday of the village, when lead was mined locally at Cwm Bychan, and the community had a blacksmith and two shops. The origins of the name Darowen are obscure. It has been suggested that it may mean 'Owain's Oaks', referring to the time when Owain Glyndwr's army was camped in the area, but this explanation lacks antiquity.

WALK 13
TAFOLWERN CASTLE MOUND

DESCRIPTION An initial steady climb on this 7-mile walk soon offers splendid views over the mountains to the south of Llanbrynmair. A gentle descent passes the old mine workings at Cwmbychan-mawr, before returning along the Twymyn valley. A short section of the route passes through some mountainside gorse, prickly for those wearing shorts! Allow 4 hours.
START From Tafolwern. SH 891027.

DIRECTIONS From the Clock Tower in Machynlleth, take the A489 east towards Newtown. At the roundabout at Cemmaes Road, take the A470 ahead. About 9 miles from Machynlleth, approaching Llanbrynmair, the road bends sharply right over the railway. The turn to Tafolwern is IMMEDIATELY to the right after the bridge. Park in Tafolwern, near the telephone box. You can take bus 522 (not Sundays) to Llanbrynmair.

1 From Tafolwern walk across the bridge and continue along the lane, passing the mound to your left. The lane climbs to the summit of a small hill, where you turn LEFT, turn RIGHT to cross a gate, and turn immediately LEFT to continue along the track, still climbing gently.

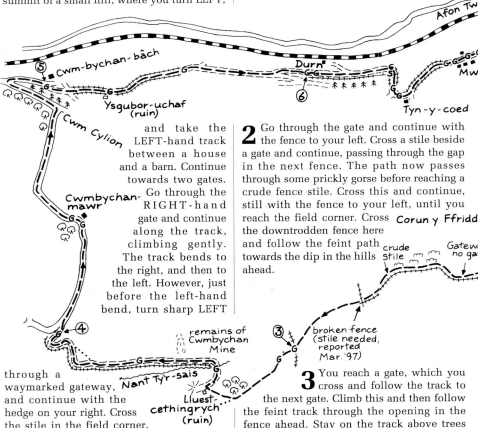

and take the LEFT-hand track between a house and a barn. Continue towards two gates. Go through the RIGHT-hand gate and continue along the track, climbing gently. The track bends to the right, and then to the left. However, just before the left-hand bend, turn sharp LEFT through a waymarked gateway, and continue with the hedge on your right. Cross the stile in the field corner,

2 Go through the gate and continue with the fence to your left. Cross a stile beside a gate and continue, passing through the gap in the next fence. The path now passes through some prickly gorse before reaching a crude fence stile. Cross this and continue, still with the fence to your left, until you reach the field corner. Cross the downtrodden fence here and follow the feint path towards the dip in the hills ahead.

3 You reach a gate, which you cross and follow the track to the next gate. Climb this and then follow the feint track through the opening in the fence ahead. Stay on the track above trees marking an old field boundary. Immediately beyond this, turn half-RIGHT downhill towards a ruin, to join a track. *There are excellent views from here.* Turn RIGHT and walk down to a gate. Go through and turn LEFT. *Up to your right are the remains of Cwmbychan lead mine. This site was probably first worked by the Romans, and was revived during the 19thC. Work ended here in 1875.* Continue along the track, passing through a gate and following it until it joins a road through another gate.

4 Maintain your direction along the road, passing through two gates at *Cwmbychan-mawr*, and following the road past

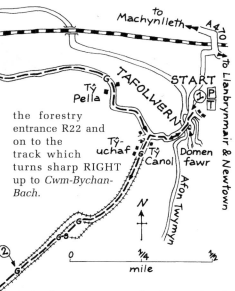

the forestry entrance R22 and on to the track which turns sharp RIGHT up to *Cwm-Bychan-Bach*.

5 At the entrance to the farm, take the RIGHT-hand gate into a field, and walk with the fence on your left. A rough track crosses as you enter an old hollow lane ahead. Continue along this hollow lane, going through a gate beside the ruins of *Ysgubor-uchaf*. The track bends to the left and eventually reaches an old wooden gate. Go through and stay on the track, ignoring a blocked track to your left. The forestry plantation has been cleared here, but just before trees appear again on your left, fork LEFT down a green track (if you reach a major

forestry road, you have gone 100yds too far!).

6 Go through two gates above the red brick house by the railway, and continue. Cross a stile beside a gate and follow the lane around to the right. Go through a gate and walk to the left, passing through another gate in front of the black-and-white house *Tyn-y-coed*. Follow the track to *Mwyars*, and continue through four gateways to join the road. Continue along the road. *Just before the road bends to the right at Ty Pella, look to the north across the valley to see Pentremawr. This was built on the site of Cynddelw Brydydd Mawr's house. He was a 12thC warrior-poet, friend of Owen Cyfeiliog (see below) and ranked amongst the best poets Europe.* Go through the gateway at *Ty Pella* and continue along the road back to the start.

*T**he mound** marks the site of Tafolwern Castle, with the cottage opposite standing in what was the open courtyard, or bailey. Originally known as Walwern, it was the home of Owen Cyfeiliog during the 12thC. A wooden building, it was described by his friend Cynddelw Brydydd Mawr (see above) as 'A'r castell eurog costwych – a costly gilded castle', and stood in the centre of what was at that time a marsh. It was granted to Cyfeiliog by Madoc ap Maredudd, last Prince of a united Powis. Cyfeiliog was a poet and one of the Princes of Powis, at a time when Powis occupied roughly what we now know as Montgomeryshire. He was on good terms with Henry II, King of England (1154-89), which did nothing to endear him to his neighbours. One of these, Hywel ab Ieuan, captured Tafolwern in 1161, but Cyfeiliog soon regained control, switching his allegiance to his over-lord Owen Gwynedd, and marrying his daughter. Together they fought against the English invasion in 1165. But the following year Cyfeiliog again switched his allegiance back to the English, and his neighbours invaded his territory in 1171. Cyfeiliog retired to Strata Marcella, and died peacefully there in 1197. Tafolwern was last mentioned in 1244 when Cyfeiliog's land was invaded by David, Prince of Gwynedd. A request was made to Henry II for fifty knights to defend the castle. The mound is private.*

WALK 14
WYNFORD'S VIEW

DESCRIPTION A 6½ mile walk which climbs steadily from Aberhosan to reach a superb viewpoint from which, on a clear day, you will see the summit of Snowdon. The descent skirts a dramatic cwm (valley), with distant views over Cardigan Bay, then continues through gentler country back to the village. Parts of this route are on an ancient track over bare rock, which can be slippery during or after wet weather. Allow 3½ hours.

START The car park below the chapel in Aberhosan. SN 810974.
DIRECTIONS From the Clock Tower in Machynlleth, take the A489 east towards Newtown, forking right opposite the 'Top Shop Chippie' towards Dylife. After 4 miles turn right as signposted to Aberhosan. As you enter the village, fork right by the chapel, and park below it, on the left. There is a post bus service from Machynlleth to Aberhosan Mon-Fri.

1 From the car park in Aberhosan, walk back up to the road by the chapel, and continue through the village. The tarmac road changes to a track, and climbs gently. Go through two gates, and continue along the track, still climbing. *Stop for a rest and look back to enjoy an extensive view.* Go through the next gate, and continue with forestry to your left. Go through another gate, and continue. Continue through the next gate to reach the Wynford Vaughan Thomas Memorial. *One of Wales' most eminent journalists and broadcasters, Wynford Vaughan Thomas identified this spot as having one of the finest views in Wales. He passed here several times whilst on his 'radio' trips through Wales on foot and horseback. The memorial was sculptured by Ieuan Rees of Llandybie. Of course it originally depicted the great man's features. He was born in 1908 in Swansea, one of three sons of a musician, and joined the BBC as an outside broadcast assistant in 1937. He became BBC War Correspondent in 1942 and never shied way from danger, making the first live broadcast from an RAF bomber over Berlin. Following the War he covered many momentous events, while finding time to make numerous radio programmes about his beloved Wales, and writing several books. Sadly missed, his infectious enthusiasm and love for his country lives on in his recordings and books.*

2 Leave the memorial through the gate onto the road, and turn RIGHT. Continue along the road for about half a mile to a track signed to 'Nature Reserve, Gwarchodle Natur'. Turn RIGHT onto this track, with Glaslyn ahead. When a track branches to the right by a waymark post, turn RIGHT here to continue the walk. *If you have time, you can continue ahead for about one-third of a mile to visit Glaslyn and the Nature Reserve. You can enjoy a ramble around the lake, but DO NOT enter the* ravine, *as it is slippery and dangerous. The track on your circular route passes to the right of the ravine, crossing bare rock which is slippery during or after wet weather, so* TAKE CARE. *On a clear day, you may be able to see Cardigan Bay from here. To the right is Foel Fadian, at 1850 ft the highest point in Montgomeryshire. The highest point on the route of this walk is 1675 ft. The track turns sharp* LEFT *at a waymark post, and descends to a gate and stile, crossing a rocky patch.*

3 Cross the stile and continue along the track, which continues its descent to another gate. Go through and carry on ahead. Pass through another gate and continue along the track to *Esgair Fochnant*, where you go through two more gates by the farm. Continue ahead.

4 Go through the gate at *Nantyfyda* and follow the road around a hairpin to the right. Go through another gateway and follow the road around to the left. When the road forks, go the RIGHT, uphill. Now stay on this road, passing through two gates at *Cefnwyrygrug*, to return to the start.

*T**he quiet little village of Aberhosan** was at one time famous for its craftsmen, who made ornamental bardic chairs for eisteddfodau, Welsh cultural festivals of music and poetry. These days it comes to life on the third Thursday in August, when it stages its annual show. There are the usual art, cookery, flower arranging and vegetable competitions, best kept pets and horse-riding, with some livelier and less tasteful games for the local lads. Aberhosan means 'mouth of the River ɩhosan'.*

to Machynlleth

②

Wynford Vaughan Thomas Memorial

to Dylife

Signpost

N

0 ¼

mile

Glyndwr's Way

Foel Fadian 1850ft ▲

Bwlch y Craig

This section is slippery when wet TAKE CARE!

Waymark Post

Waymark Post

Cwm Hafod March

Nant Fadian

Glyndwr's Way

③ Afon Dulas

Uwch-y-coed

Glaslyn

WALK 15
WATERFALLS OVER PENNANT

DESCRIPTION A steep descent and an even steeper climb make this an energetic and exciting 5½ mile walk. The rewards for your efforts are stunning views, fine waterfalls and a friendly pub to relax in when you return. However, because of the strenuous nature of this walk, which involves a short, steep section of descent on the outward route, a stream to cross, and a 650-foot climb within about 600 yards on the return, we could not recommend this walk to those with very young children, or those who would not be happy negotiating the steep descent and ascent There are, however, no sheer drops by the path, and those who make the effort will enjoy a *quite exceptional* walk. Allow 3 ½ hours.

START From the Star Inn, Dylife, but don't park right by the pub if you are not intending to visit. There is plenty of parking space at Dylife. SN 863941.

DIRECTIONS From the Clock Tower in Machynlleth, take the A489 east towards Newtown, forking right opposite the 'Top Shop Chippie' towards Dylife. At Dylife, turn left to park close to the Star Inn.

1 From the Star Inn, walk back to the main road and turn LEFT. Walk along to the head of the valley. *You get a good view of the Ffrwdd Fawr waterfall from here, and a notice board explains that the River Twymyn used to flow from east to west before the last ice age, when a glacier scoured out a 'U' shaped valley. When the ice melted the river changed course and eroded the valley into the 'V' shape we can see. The water falls almost 200 ft, making this cascade one of Wales' highest.* Continue along the road to just beyond a group of conifers, where a track branches to the LEFT. Go through the gate and follow the track. *There are splendid views to the west.*

2 The track forks at two gates. Go through the LEFT-hand gate, but DO NOT follow the clear track ahead. Walk to the LEFT across the grass, to find the clear path which starts to descend steeply. *TAKE GREAT CARE ON THIS INITIAL STRETCH OF PATH.* The short rocky section is soon passed, and the descent becomes more gentle. Maintain your direction downhill, and the path soon becomes a fine green lane. Go through the gate at *Pennant-uchaf* and continue to *Pennant-isaf*, where you pass through four gates and continue along the lane. Cross the bridge at Pentre Cilcwm and pass the new bungalow on the left.

3 Turn LEFT up the track to *Cilcwm-fawr*, but DO NOT enter the yard. Instead, go through a gate on the RIGHT, cross a small enclosure and go through a second, way-marked, gate. Turn LEFT and walk up to a third gate, which you go through, continuing ahead, with a fence on the left. Go through a gate ahead, then walk downhill, with a fence on your left. Cross a small stile and continue, now with the fence to your right, and the Afon Twymyn to your left. Cross a small stream, pass a redundant stile and continue. Go through gate ahead, and carry on along the path beside the Twymyn, going through another gate and negotiating muddy patches.

4 The rough path crosses a stream. This can be a little wide after rainfall, so step carefully on stones to keep your feet dry! Now veer to the RIGHT to a gate. Go through and continue uphill, passing a waymark on a tree to the left. Go through the gate ahead and begin the climb up the very steep path, which zig-zags up the mountainside. *Stop regularly to enjoy the splendid views from this path, and catch your breath.*

5 Eventually you reach a stile. Cross it and continue, with the fence to your right. You soon drop down to a stream. Cross the bridge and go through the gate ahead (ignoring the gate further to the right) and turn LEFT up the track. Go through the next gate and walk towards the right hand side of Capel Seion ahead. Go through the gate beside the chapel and continue along the tarmac lane, to return to the Star Inn, for a well earned pint (or whatever you fancy).

While you are relaxing in the Star Inn, or returning from your walk, you can reflect upon what changes have been wrought in little over 100 years, for in the mid and late 1800s the population of Dylife, 'the place of floods', numbered around 1000, and the mines were amongst the most productive in Wales. Originally worked by the Romans, the mines reached the peak of their production in 1863, when 2571 tons of lead ore were recovered. Over 250 miners were employed, and Dylife had several pubs, a school, post office, church and chapels. It was the discovery of the Llechwedd Ddu lode which brought about the mines' most productive period, initially under the ownership of Williams & Pughe, who carted the ore 14 hilly miles to the port of Derwenlas (see Walk 9) for transhipment. By this time the mine was large enough to admit horses, pulling small wagons on tracks. Several reservoirs were constructed, one of which powered the Martha Wheel, which with a 63 ft diameter was the largest ever built in Wales. Cobden & Bright (Richard Cobden was an exponent of free trade and campaigned for the abolition of the corn laws) bought the mine in 1858 for £24,000, re-equipping to such an extent that it could claim to be the most modern in the country. Output began falling in 1871, but such was the mines' reputation that the Great Dylife Company took it over in 1873. Today little remains to remind us of this once great enterprise.

WELSH

The meanings of some of the common words found in local place names

aber	mouth	**garth**	enclosure, hill
afon	river, stream	**glas**	green, blue
allt	hillside	**glyder**	heap
		glyn	glen
bach	small	**gors**	bog
banc	hill	**grug**	heather
blaen	head of valley	**gwen**	white
bont	bridge	**gyrn**	peak
bryn	hill		
bwlch	pass	**hafod**	summer dwelling
		hen	old
cadair (cader)	chair	**hendre**	winter dwelling
caer	fort	**heol**	road
capel	chapel	**hir**	long
castell	castle		
cefn	ridge	**isaf**	lowest
ceunant	ravine		
coch	red	**llan**	church
coed	wood	**llech**	slate
craig	rock	**llidiart**	gate
croes	cross	**llwyd**	grey
cwm	valley	**llyn**	lake
dinas	fort, city	**maen**	stone
dol	meadow	**maes**	field
du	black	**mawr**	big
dwr	water	**melin**	mill
dyffryn	valley	**moch**	pigs
		moel	bare hill
eglwys	church	**mor**	sea
esgair	hillspur	**mynach**	monk
		mynydd	mountain
fach	small		
fan	high place	**nant**	stream
fawr	large	**neuadd**	hall
fechan	small	**newydd**	new
felin	mill		
ffordd	road	**ogof**	cave
ffynnon	spring, well		
foel	bare hill		
fynydd	mountain		

pandy	mill
pant	hollow
parc	field, park
pen	top
penmaen	rocky headland
pistyll	waterfall, spout
plas	mansion
porth	port
pwll	pool
rhaeadr	waterfall
rhiw	hill
rhos	marsh, moor
rhyd	ford
sarn	road
sych	dry
tarren	hill
tomen	mound
traeth	shore, beach
traws	across
tref	hamlet, home
twll	hole
ty	house
uchaf	highest
y, yr	the, of the
ynys	island
ysgol	school
ystrad	valley floor